And If the Woods Carry You

Also by Erin Rodoni

Body, in Good Light

A Landscape for Loss

And If the Woods Carry You

Erin Rodoni

Winner of the 2020 Michael Waters Poetry Prize

Southern
Indiana
Review
Press

Published by the University of Southern Indiana
Evansville, Indiana

ISBN 978-1-930508-51-4   First Edition

Printed in the USA

Library of Congress Control Number: 2021940773

This publication is made possible by the support of the Indiana Arts Commission, the National Endowment for the Arts, the University of Southern Indiana College of Liberal Arts, the USI English Department, the USI Foundation, and the USI Society for Arts & Humanities.

Southern Indiana Review Press
Orr Center #2009
University of Southern Indiana
8600 University Boulevard
Evansville, Indiana 47712

sir.press@usi.edu
usi.edu/sir
Ron Mitchell, Rosalie Moffett, and Marcus Wicker, eds.

Cover art: Chie Yoshii; *Memento Mori*, 2016; *chieyoshii.com*
Cover design: Zach Weigand

for my family

CONTENTS

The Woods

The Village

The Kingdom

The Clearing

Stay where you are poor beast, this is no world for you.

–Peter S. Beagle, *The Last Unicorn*

THE WOODS

LULLABY WITH FIREFLIES AND RISING SEAS

And if the woods carry you into their deep
and tangled. If the woods claim you

elf or sprite and spirit you
from me. Tell me your first fireflies

were enough, the lawn they candled
to enchantment. Because the dark

of childhood is mythed
and monstered, but my dark

mind glints off every surface
sharp enough to slit. Tonight,

ice sheets slide like seals
into the sea and in Nice,

parents hurl their children out
of the truck's path. Their only

prayer, a heartbeat's worth
of *please*. Maybe, like me,

the only god you can conceive
is a kind of wakefulness.

Feel the stream of night
tugging your ankles? See

the seams of night
torn with those brief lights?

Sometimes I ring
the fine bones of your wrist

with my forefinger and thumb
and wonder at the monstrous

love that flung you into this.
In every fairy tale, the mother dies

and is replaced by someone wicked. It's true,
I want to keep you safe, but I want

to keep you mine. I never meant to fly
you like a kite. I never meant to stay

behind. But the mother is a cottage
the daughter flutters from, the mother

more cage than bird, and the parting clean
as a licked sword. The future, a castle that can't be

childproofed. And the fairy tale, still
open on my lap, is not a map.

Growing Up Wild

Look how tall the pines loom,
how deep glacial streams gash
fields of lupine. It is dangerous
to be a child. The starcut wilds spark
with rhythms and nothing rhymes
when her griefcry cracks
the Precambrian sky, a blue so ancient
I almost believe humans will never
touch it. But we are worming
up there too, parasites grazing
the mind of God. There is so little left
untouched and god knows we can't stop
touching. I hurry my babies along
wellmarked trails in wellmapped
woods, through a camouflaged dazzle
of song. A doe stills us with her side-
eye while her fawns fleet into the trees.
So many creatures slide from
our gaze, little flames of meeting.
No matter how much I wish this
swordsheen green for us, the *Timber!*
shadows laying down the planks
of coming night, no matter how much
I want those arctic stars, swarmed thick
against a black that seems somehow plush
and vacant at once, sometimes I fear there
is nowhere safer to keep the wild
than outside. Any territory, I'm told,
once claimed, must be defended. So we kill
even with our desire to live
gently. But there is no gentleness
between hunger and what feeds
it. Oh, it is dangerous
to love a child.

Time Capsule: The Fallow Deer

Reader, they have slaughtered the white deer of my childhood.
My father enchanted them into unicorns as they drifted in with the fog

that filled our valleys. They were imports, ornamental. Shipped in
by some rich eccentric for his pleasure. Reader, it's true: they outgrew

their pen, outlived their keeper. Up close they were not white, really, more day-
old snow, their fur matted with ticks and burrs. Their horns not spiral,

but branched. Reader, they were nothing like unicorns, but I loved
to spot them from my father's truck as we drove the sinuous

road to the coast. How they came out like stars in the scrub oak.
My father kept a gun in the back seat. He kept a season for killing,

the other three for wonder. I woke once to headlights
slashed across my bedroom window, a buck strung

by his hind legs in the pear tree, belly split sternum to pelvis,
my father cutting him down into pieces we could swallow.

Those evenings though, my father never fired, only whistled
to startle them up from their grazing so I could call them

by their horns: button buck, spike, doe. They called them invasive
and shot them from helicopters. Who were they, Reader, to draw

the line of belonging? The white deer were my fireflies,
my everyday magic. But who am I? In the crackle of starlight,

above dry leaves soaked silent, the dead buck shone, nothing
like a unicorn. Up close it is harder to stomach what we do

with this awe, with these hands.

HUNTRESS

The stag's heart spoke (as it passed
through my throat) of desire.

I've held the strangest of strangers.
To swallow, the quickest way to close

that distance. I'm still so hungry for
the tribe of shadows that rubs

its fur against my nighttime
and there are no bars, but bars

of trees. Yes, the forest speaks
with many voices.

All of them say *Lie down,*
die here. Yes, stomachs split

and organs fall from
ordained order. A liver jewels

at me through the murk
of dream. All beings fall

through each other, through topsoil,
into deep cradles of rain.

I'm afraid I'll never know another
body, only the bloom

of impact. And in the dark
we're all moonblind, heat-

seeking. I've seen the cavity-
colored tracks in antlers,

ticks balloon with blood,
and fleas rise like ghosts from drying

hides. How deep I've looked
with my gleaming knives.

Their eyes are open,
but their gaze is closed.

Like them, I've learned to veil
my face in breath, white as vapor-

bone. Behind it, my teeth
press my tongue until I can taste

my own blood, the tang of steel
bars in the rain.

Oh Artemis,

I did all the things you wouldn't. My heart beat
to be snared. And it was, and it was. Oh capture
of glances. Hot stammer of graces

against my neck, my breasts. Oh love, that trap.
I am heavy with it. My hips laden with daughters.
Settled, domestic. Artemis, my girls are all sinew

and shine. And heathen still. Your dystopian
disciples, they crest the ridge of the future,
mooncaged and clad in what they have killed.

Flintstrike of foot against forest floor. See
how they sharpen, laureled with breath? I whisper
such myth into their skin while they sleep

beneath tree limbs. In the shadow-
lace of leaves, wilds dart beneath their eyelids.
Still, they run screaming from spiders,

even as the cellar stocks with canned goods
and the age of play swings toward its end.
Still, bloodshed remains

something that happens on the moon-
bleached highway while they dream.
On the way to school, I see their eyes

in the rearview mirror, follow a stain
to the side of the road, where some poor
nocturnal creature spills her guts

in brutish sun. Day after day she decays
like an omen of what is to come. Oh Artemis,
you were my favorite. I should have run.

ON BEING OUT OF THE WOODS

They don't tell you the woods are like the universe:
infinite, and expanding. There is no getting out.
You can only weave between the trees. Outrun
the cones exploding into growth. The compass spins,
dear so-and-so. Branches blacker than night
smack the guiding star about, an errant firefly.
They don't tell you the woods are like the past:
haunted, and evergreen. There is no forgetting.
To forgive is to move. Away or toward? Memory,
eyes in the dark. Memory, a clearing. Dear so-and-so,
as you may have guessed, to be woodbound is to be
bound to every risk. May the wolf howl only
in the distance, the rustling be but the waking
of owls in the gables of dusk. Born to hunt,
reared on luck. They don't say the woods
will make you prey. May the wings slapping above
be but fruit bats, sugarseekers with no lust for blood.
It's okay to pray. Defenseless, you fill with reverence:
these wedded roots, the leafstrung lute, the wind
that strums the same damned seasons, cyclic
and scything. To breathe is to feel the dead inside you
rising. Dear so-and-so, let me tell you, the woods
are like love. The most beautiful place
you'll ever be. And terrifying.

TEST

I know the symptoms—nausea,
swollen lymph nodes, a phantom

       dread—could indicate a thousand
       benign things, but it was the worst thing,

and too late. I know better
than to ask a woman, no matter

       how globelike, if she's pregnant,
       no matter how coupled and cloudlike,

when she will, if she wants to have,
and how many. I know a woman

       who had given up on love. She fell
       late and completely with a man

who loved the sea. His heart
stopped on a boat beneath a

       clot of gulls and she was nowhere
       near and is now growing old

alone as she had planned,
but sadder. I know there

       are worse things, far
       worse endings. I know

surgery can save us,
that the solid state

       of blood is scab, then
       skin, but even healing

has its complications.
I know each breath is a bargain

we make with later
and that deaths do come in threes,

and fives, and thousands.
I know we will still rejoice

at the unburial of a single
miracle. After the miscarriage

(I know there are worse
beginnings), and the trying,

the trying, after making it
through the first trimester,

finally, when they said chance,
when they said one in three,

your baby, I thought *Life
cannot possibly be this cruel.*

And it wasn't,
but I know it is.

THE POEM BEGINS WITH US SURVIVING

the collapse, the mass extinction, in the clearing
of an everafter. The poem fairytales the little cottage,
the silver stream. A trail of crumbs, snow-
white in redwoods, guides us homeward
from our daily scavenging. We could live there
couldn't we? For whatever forever
we have left? But I can't get past the damn blood
my daughter needs transfused into her veins.
Once she woke ashen, blue edged her lips.
They said *Yes bring her, bring her quick.*
We were two hours from the hospital, and the poem stalls
while I remember that drive through the false dusk
of redwoods, the daggers of sunlight I squinted against,
trying not to submit to the thicket of panic.
What if the hospital were a ruin
of vermin and vine? The phone lines choked
with lichen. Our trail of crumbs indistinguishable
from ash. In the shadow of an everafter,
the desperate parent submits to the terms
of the witch. The life-for-life trade, for
mercy, for magic. The poem bewitches.
I could pierce my own artery and not pass out.
Recite a spell to charm my blood serpentine.
Or to summon a wolf. In the poem, he lowers
his heart to my blade. In the poem, it beats
the blush back to her cheeks. Yes, I can write that
fierce moonlight, prowl of star on ice, right
into her bloodstream. But the poem always ends
with the princess white as snow. It is winter.
We are more alone than we have ever been.

To Never Have Been

Of reincarnation my husband said *Imagine the horror
of being a baby again.* I saw only babies

paraded in prams like tiny monarchs
and didn't understand.

Then summer came with its terrible heat
inside locked cars.

The logic of oblivion is irresistible.
If a thing does not exist it cannot suffer.

But wouldn't I miss this suffering?
The strip mall stricken with sunlight.

How the deathache in my chest
bolts awake. The baby cries

and no one comes. I don't want to think
about the heat. A belief

in past lives is a belief in connection.
The baby forgotten in the car

was once the mother remembering
with a bolt of adrenaline

hours later at her desk. My husband explains
The law of karma is that we must suffer

our every desire. The mercy lies
in portion size. The suffering

is spread over many lives
so it cannot destroy us.

So every life destroys us a little
at a time. I don't want to speak

of what the mother finds.
In this life I remember

the baby with the bolt
of the lock. A terrible heat

feeds distant fires, casts the sun
an otherworldly pink. A bolt of beauty

unlocks an ageless ache.
The baby sleeps through the moment

she was almost, but not,
left. If we rise and fall

from the same source,
why rise at all? I want to say to suffer

love, but my logic goes all loopy,
keeps chasing its tail. Maybe all logic

is circular. Maybe there is no oblivion
but this.

FORGIVE ME, I'VE FORGOTTEN

how to be a daughter. I am all forest now. I surround my
     daughter in green shadow. A kind of absence. She knows me as throat-

     hum, a dull ache. Mother, forgive these trees, this doe-
eyed girl. She is lost and I keep losing

my place. Like an infant, like a corpse, I sleep
     flat on my back. I am on your lap. I am the meadow grass,

     the clearing, the songcharmed beasts. Dreams like moving water
ripple your face above my face. The light subterranean,

as if through skin. The forest thickens with cries
     from a baby I cannot find. Perhaps she's the daughter

     I once was, the one who grew away from you.
Perhaps she's the daughter who slips

her braided lies through my hair like soothing fingers.
     Hear the echo there, the water moving? It carries the crying

     deep inside the past, which is my body,
which is your body, where it quiets

into a fawn, earthdrawn and downtongued. The lips
     of a stream open to her kiss the way the heart does,

     gently. Mother, I remember pinching the skin
of your knuckles, amazed at how long it steepled

while my own snapped back. That once-
     magic flattened into lack, of collagen, elastin. Love grows from,

     then away from, the body. I am in a forest. A blue-
white doe hovers like a butane flame.

In velvet vowels, she hums her warning.
     Perhaps it's the same lullaby

you plaited with the sound of rain. The same
my daughter whispersings without knowing why

when she's afraid. I am afraid.
The forest thins like aging skin.

BURY ME IN THE WOODS OF MY CHILDHOOD

As a child I pledged myself to a tree,
a walnut in the backyard I called mine,

my tree, though it wasn't
as presumptuous as it sounds.

It was just I didn't know a word
for what I felt for the tree

and there was no word for whatever it felt
for me, the girl who grazed her knees

daily on its silver bark. The girl who hugged
with her whole body, who closed her eyes

and listened to the humming of leaf and limb,
the aura of insect and birdchatter in its crown,

my private galaxy of sound.
Against my cheek, my tree was comfort

to the small muscles in my jaw,
forever smoothing the world

into something I could stomach. Theirs is
a slow time, of creaks and groans and sways,

and when I lived there I was slow too. I remained
a girl, though I grew older, long-

limbed and limber, my weight feline
in its languor. How I loved the leaves where coolness

lingered as sun lit up the veins inside, and I pressed
my palm against one as if it were a hand, as if to say

There is something now between us, my own ancient.
I was alive. I was in time, drifting as I was the afternoon

entire, cradled but not sleeping, rocking but not
a single bough breaking, not a crack. So awfully

tender, so full of sap. I wonder if the tree
remembers me. I wonder if it asks where

I have gone, and the network of fungi beneath
my feet lights up with my footsteps, relaying

with the symmetry of synapse: *She is here.*
She grows heavy, then light again.

THE VILLAGE

I WAS THE GIRL WHO JUMPED FIRST

into the sanest danger, from ledges a sensible
length above the creek, tide just high enough
to cover the mundane wreckage of small-
town reckless—Chevys and shopping carts, corpse-
cows fat with fermented clover—down
deep where currents creep, quick
and colder. There, sunk in the silt: the girl,
the ghost, the gift my country spooked
me with. Two towns over, she vanished
from her bed or was rumored rotten in man-
tall grass by moonlicked railroad tracks.
The prologue always the same: she wandered,
she strayed from. Yes, fear twice removed
is fear. I grew into the girl who never stayed
past curfew. Always drove myself so I'd
never have to owe or beg my way. Accelerated
out of every turn in my mother's roll-
prone Jeep. Protected by a physics barely
grasped, I circled risk beneath those fog-
dulled stars. I never took a goddamn thing too far.

Time Capsule: The Cross Beside the Creek

The blackberries are red
and hard. The creek is flat,

       the breeze. A hushed calligraphy
       of reeds. Cattails too still to trace

the warning that hovers
just beneath the shine. The plaque

       is rusted now and rippled. *In Memory*,
       I trace. A name. Two dates. She was nine

when she drowned in this same muddy pool
I teach my girl to swim in now. She floats above

       my hands, an ordinary levitation.
       A displacement. No moment goes

unhaunted. My friend, looking straight ahead,
whispers how a man she'd trusted forced her

       right out of her own skin—*like I was floating.*
       The summer before, we'd squatted

in the shallows, concocting love
potions of bronze water and smashed leaves.

       Girl Scout mantras kept us safe—*Leaves of three
       leave it be; stem so smooth with purple streaks*—

My daughter startles at her sudden weight-
lessness, thrashes as she sinks

       back into my waiting hands.
       Beyond the reeds, a wreath

of hemlock, or Queen Anne's lace. *Stem so smooth*—
Flowers white—I can't for the life of me

recall that final rhyme,
divining crown from killer.

Maybe It Was Summer

Maybe I was in love. Maybe Summer Crush was a blush
I wore to complement chlorine streaks in my hair.

It was the year the little girl drowned in our town's sweet
little creek. Or it was the year after, when the little-

girl panties were found somewhere they shouldn't be.
Details fade, but a slippery darkness clings to the underside

of leaves. There were whispers among the grownups
or the children dreamed of empty swings, pushed

by a bloodrush breeze. It might have been the season
of coffee ice cream and clove cigarettes. Maybe the smoke

seasicked my gut like a crush. Maybe there were two girls
and a boy. I know I was always the third body,

the one not being touched. Maybe invisibility is a power,
but it felt more like a curse. There may have been a man

camped on the banks of the creek, beard dreaded
and burred. He might have fought in Vietnam,

but it might have been Iraq. Maybe it was June,
and we were told to stay away from him. No,

it was Independence Day and there were gunshots
in the abandoned building. Maybe it had been empty

for centuries. Maybe they never found his body
or maybe he left town. Maybe I can't turn on the lamp

of what happened without illuminating everything
that could have. The lamp was my torso,

stamped to the boy's window, or the night above
his bed was heavy with my wanting so he slept little,

and then less. Maybe he was helplessly out of love
and I was heartless. It might have been the decade of war

in a distant country. Or a decade later, when the war
was not so distant but felt no closer than before.

It was the era of wildfire. It was the age of oil in the
estuary. Maybe it doesn't matter if it was grease or

soot. Birds were snared in something slick and patent-
black. Maybe it wasn't summer proper, but the

September sibling that flares before the leaves
begin to fall. Maybe the huckleberries were ripe

or maybe sicksweet. Maybe they were plump
as ticks and I burst them between my thumb and finger

one by one. There was the wind of rust
or the wind of slaughter. There was a sickle

moon, a harvest moon. I think I saw a sodden sun
and a glassfloat moon, bobbing on opposite horizons.

Maybe it was a scale I couldn't balance, so I shrunk
the world to background until I became the star.

Maybe the sun had set already into a lacquered sea,
beach fires scooping out the night, the dark packed

hard between them. Maybe the dark between was dense
enough to scald, and the glow, like a bioluminescent lure,

reminded me of warmth, but wasn't
warm at all.

TIME CAPSULE: THE UNEVEN FIELD

Yes, I went to the field like a virgin   to the mouth of a volcano,

meaning I was in love   with my ornaments: the jeweled tug   at my lobes, the gold

          squeeze at my throat.   Each pulse, the secret hollow   behind

each ear, swooned   with sandalwood and slumber.   Grasshoppers

slammed themselves against my bare midriff.   Yes, I came to gather eyes

          like moths.   I came despite. I knew   the common root

of sacrifice   and sacrament.   It was a rite   of passage,   to be named

for the part that beckoned best.   Yes, I went to the field like a bride

drunk on dowry,   all that worth, all that sparkle   in his stare.   Yes, I wanted

to be watched,   thus christened. Yes,   other girls returned, shining

          like the moon,   by which I mean on the other side

of that romanticized light,   there is a dark   treeline   where anything could hide.

          Husk of daylight   heavening the sky.

Fragrance of wild   vines coiling   barbed wire, blossoming   small white stars

          named Jasmine, Honeysuckle.   Hush:

the field was a body   of water. I learned to float   by holding still. The field

was a mirror that returned my body to me   through his eyes.   No, the field was a body

of water, and I kept sinking   through my own reflection.   The slightest scramble

          between sacred   and scared. Aware

suddenly of the cold   in my cutoffs and croptop. Sheer, the drop.   No, I didn't fall   for him.

If I burned,   it was for beauty. That plummet   through the manystoried night.

Immolation Lessons

Let these wives first step into the pyre, tearless without any affliction and well adorned.

–Sati hymn, *Rig Veda*

A finger's width is touch enough to tender
    a girl unused to glowing at the center

        of attention. She'll fill that space, a show
pony hoofing inanities in tight dressage,

        until something in her finches, dizzy with
            insistence. The prick of a lit wick.

        Before Sati was an act
she was a daughter who defied

her father for a god too cool to notice
    her devotion, until it was consummate.

    Now she knows better
        than to look at what their eyes are

mouthing, keeps her shoulders stiff,
    as if the touch is unwanted or wanted

    too much. It's a slow dance with a wind
        she's half afraid of. Each feathery fingertip promises

quill, pinches like boys on Saint Patrick's when girls
    on purpose don't wear green. Nothing's worse

    than to be unseen. As tripwire chakras
        explode her spine from coccyx

        to hairline in controlled demolition,
Sati cries *Papa, I enter his heart*

    in a suicide vest. In a vacuum
a feather plummets at the rate of

I can't take it anymore. Such surrender,
        is it strength? I'll cheat and say that it depends

on what it's to. We've adorned our flesh
        to keep the spirit clothed.

We've burned the clothes
        to let our spirit show.

PRESERVATION LESSONS

My daughter looks at her hands   for a long time. After
I tell her what they can do.   To anyone who tries

     to take her. The girl doesn't want   a stranger's blood
     beneath her nails, doesn't want   the shocking give

of a stranger's eye.   I took my first self-
defense class   when I was eleven. I still can't

     shake the cringe.   The girl makes a fist.
     Thumb tucked   inside. I shake

my head. Pull her   fingers sharp.
The lamp casts   our shadows on the wall.

     The shadow mother   merges with the shadow
     daughter. It goes on   forever.

What a hand knows   of forever: bone. And
grip. Hold hands to stay   together. Not to

     lose. To squeeze.   A warning. An accident,
     averted.   Yanked from the grasp

of disaster. Such small hands.   Busy always.
Scribbling crayons into nubs.   Melting chocolate.

     Impossibly quick.   The chance between hesitate
     and too late.   My hand rakes snarls

from her curls.   A shadow hand catches her
ponytail. Yanks   her chin straight up.

     Her throat   exposed. And all
     the tiny roots sing   *Ouch!*

I know it hurts.   I know. These hands
soothe. Wound their own   palms with their own

nails. With rage. With worry. I look at the dirt
beneath her nails. See blood. My hands

guide hers. Dagger. Bludgeon. Gouge.
The lamp casts shadows on the wall. Rabbit.

Danger. *Run!* The girl memorizes
the shapes her hands must make if

she is caught. Behind the shapes,
the violence. Of what her hands can do

if they have to. To escape. And beyond
escape, the violence. Why she has to.

Time Capsule: Days of Ash from Elsewhere

And the indoor play

        gets darker. Dolls fever-red,   leech-bled. Pocked radiant

with Crayola.
        Tissue-wrapped, bed-ridden.

Dolls maimed in scissor-jaws,   monster claws, the moon's

mute maw.   Dolls slack in the back

        of a speeding ambulance.

Vampire-attacked. Raptor-   slashed, stripped   and hacked.

    Vanished for the bluest hour.

        Searched for, forsaken.   The game hangs

on my daughter's whim

      which today tips toward
        salvation. We dredge the quarry,

salt the leeches thin. Undress   the wounds, redress the torsos

in sequin and chiffon. We reattach

      the limbs, press every head   back on. We raise the dead.

Understand?
    We raise them.

THE KINGDOM

In God's Image We Are Arsonists

Fire was our first magic,

        our best trick. Almost domestic,

how like a just-

        hatched chick it trembled in our hands—

                No mother ever made a monster

                    who didn't dare

                to love her back.

Children grow

        in a blink, they say.

But stars explode

        so slow they never change.

                And if she wakes

                    to find her little monster

                has loosed a plague

should we blame the hand

        that made the hand

or the hand that lit the flame?

Parable of the Bull

They passed down all the roads long ago, and the Red Bull ran close behind them and covered their footprints.

–Peter S. Beagle, *The Last Unicorn*

I. We decide to vanish

when fire meets flood, our backs to the sea and nowhere to run. I am in the middle of a life. I have lived half a life in the Lord's gated pastures, their sprinklers and sprawl. The children do not deserve their suffering, but perhaps I do. Perhaps a noxious mix of guilt and horror warps the inferno into the spectre of a bull. The red gaze charging, charging us with arson, delusions of grandeur, grand larceny of grandest redwoods. How dare we bilk such silver brooks to boil, fleece the very air with choke and hack. The trash of eons ignites into horns, forcing us back and back. For a time, I am a mother and the trees seem to huddle away from us, as if they are a herd. Or a single furred and flinching being; I think I hear it gasp like a diver preparing to submerge. Waves lap our knees. In the sea I am a child. My mother slips from me, but there are others to hold onto. In the sea we billow and bump against each other, swell with salt. Permeable, algae blooms inside us, lengthening our limbs. Our too-soft skin gums together and I feel the smother of each cell in our shared lungs. We drift here forever, scumming the tide with our lye. The frail kings, who finally own everything, watch us from golden balconies, until heat meets melting point. All the while, the bull brightens like something holy or hellish, then flickers out. When the waves peel back, we stand on ash. I am no longer young. I am older than I deserve to be. In the sudden clarity of stars I remember each purchase, each plunder. I am so ancient by now, I know our God of bribery and vengeance, our Lord of pediatric cancer and private jets, is also the wind that whips the flames, is also the bull, hurling its heft against the waves. The bull whirling in our red weather. The sun itself when it floods its red right through us.

II. Parameters of the Parable

For the sake of the poem, the decision cannot be reversed.
The means remain hazy.

Perhaps a sterilizing drug is administered at birth.
Or an aerosol dispersed via satellite

across the earth. We must assume suffering.
We must assume the innocent suffer first,

and more than the guilty. Yes, they still charge
with desire to hold something small

and good, but those who remain
have just one power left: refusal

to manifest hope
into flesh.

III. The Last Mother

But there are still days we have everything we need.
Beauty, a solid acre of it. A summer that never ends.

Summer fields scorched copper and crimson.
This garden of fire-hued leaves still glistens

with nightshades: tomato, aubergine. Skin,
dust, and sun. My little tuber, you seem all eyes,

though the two on your head barely see. Your pupils hover
the way I imagine my face must, a watery planet

you almost remember. You are so still
it seems you could live on light. It loves you,

light; it lights upon you like a butterfly
a flower. Of course you open your mouth

expecting Eden. My milk, the last manna.
My hands, dry as the creek bed.

These nights, we sleep tangled
and dreamwrecked. These mornings,

already heavy with ghosts and dead bees.
The season so full already, but somehow with room

to swallow us too. In this fool's September,
even the shadows are golden, the pears

tearing with the weight of their hips.
Oh endling, I flood at the trembling

of your lower lip. Aren't we still blessed
here in our banishment?

IV. The Last Babies Are Stars

Meaning they are famous.

The last babies have millions of fans.

Everything they do goes

viral. The last first

smile. The last

first word. The last first step.

We track our vanishing

by their growth charts.

We celebrate

and mourn their birthdays,

until they are old

enough to remind us of ourselves

and we have to look away.

They are stars,

meaning they are beautiful

ghosts, meaning their light

is of the past,

meaning it shines

out from a gone place.

They are stars, meaning made

of stardust. Meaning dust

to dust and dust to something

that is not us. The last

babies are stars meaning

How we wish—

V. The Last Generation of Children Inherits the Earth

The old books speak of schools
      of fish, numerous
as ripples, each flick of light, a fin,
      a tail. Of herds, flooding

the plain with their thunder,
      flocks dimming the day
like an eclipse. Of earth
      soft, fertile and loaded

with biomass, all for us.
      Now everything is waterlogged,
rotten, an abundance
      that does not feed us.

The tundra fizzes
      to life. All that is not us
bubbles up around us,
      effervescent, hungry

for our every exhalation.
      Bunkered beneath
glacial runoff,
      we sprout heirloom seeds

in our hot mouths. Then chew.
      Bestsellers warn of The Bull
as they cool into lore
      in our flickering hands.

⁄⁄

                The old myths of our resurrection
         are outdone

                by blackened stumps periscoping
         tiny shoots, up and up.

When the balance is right,
the coiled roots hiss:

Let there be green.
And the whole world springs.

❧

We learn about creation
        by the way nature reclaims the light. The canopy
closes above us.

We fall
        more and more into silence. The white noise of treetalk
cottons our memories of traffic,

        and the sea scrubs the land of our wars,
our wonders. All the carbon in the air
        drives the green things wild, makes us sick

and quiet. The forests flare
        into each other, charge
through the cities.

        The environment is hostile
and we are hostage
        to the penthouse suite, just before

the tower crumbles. We waltz
        in castles that might as well be clouds.
Indulge our tinsel and our crowns.

VI. On the verge of our vanishing, the world

becomes beautiful again.   A great greening   writhes through the lands

we wasted   with claiming.   Bright pheromones bribe us   to abandon

the past where it stands.   There is no one left   to raise, nothing to pass

down, so we pass it back   and forth between us.   No one follows

in our footsteps,   so we dance.

❦

The forest is kingdom, empire   entire, and we are always on our knees.

     Our prey   whitens with the snow.   Its vanishing outruns us.

          Nature takes back   whatever we can no longer hold,

the way the wind lifts leaves that lighten   with dying. Its touch

not unkind,   but no kind at all.

VII. Eve, Alone

Say the last human ever born
is female. Say she outlives the last

of men. Let us call her Eve and wish her
a year or two on Earth without the gaze of any

Adam. Let her devour the fruit of any tree
she pleases. Whatever wisdom sparkles

in the sugar, let her chew in the cherish
of her own mind. Above, the trees speak blossom,

birdsong. Eve has begotten no one, is beguiled
by all she sees. Below her, a slower synapse

inches, root-tip to root-tip. The forest abides
no border but the desert and the sea.

Eve touches the heads of the animals.
Their names flash in her brain

before vanishing. At daybreak, at nightfall,
she releases every verse and prayer

ever captured from the prismed air.
When Eve falls, a rapture

of insects shrouds her body.
Scavengers disrobe. Microbes unchristen

to the bone. The whole web of creation
crackles with her as she rises

into the crown of Ash,
of Alder. Birch, River and Silver.

Cedar and Elm. Lord,
the names are so beautiful. The woman, more

striking for being called Eve. Of course, Eden
was always made of language, never trees.

VIII. Eden, After

And once   the great flank of devastation   has brushed past,

if better natures   phoenix from the ash,

if what comes next is a clearing   cauled in Eden's dew. A clearing

still charged   with threats   the trees sense.

It is as if someone has just left,   or is about to   be born.

Some unspeakable   spoken, some rocks broken

against each other. In the space between   crack and spark,

silence rings   an octave sharper   than it should.

The leaves vibrate   like cochleas.   The leaves capture like corneas.

A million flashes   of our absence   amber in branches,

worm into roots. Thin out and squirm   through the soil.

Even gods dissolve.   Even every last miracle

that made us.

LAST UNICORNS

If I had two lives to live, would I
live one without you? In the quiet

living room, I was once alone
watching *The Last Unicorn*

all afternoon, my mother unseen
in her closed bedroom.

It frightened me
how the forest vanished

from the unicorn's ageless eyes
when she fell in love, becoming

fully maiden. The rug I crosslegged on
was a copy of a tapestry my mother loved

when she was young and not
mine. Unicorn and maiden intertwined

with flowered vines. How desperately I rooted
for her to return to her unicorn form

and to her forest, to live forever
in the magic that kept the world around her

evergreen, and distant. It frightened me
when the unicorn-turned-maiden cried

I can feel this body dying all around me!
I wished so hard then for a clearing

in which I might be spared
by being chosen.

Once, my mother went alone to a museum
to see *The Lady and the Unicorn* tapestries

and came home with forest flickering her eyes.
I could almost smell the stars there,

in her other life: chalk and ash, distance,
and how they burn to stay

alight, as if it cost nothing. I wanted
so badly to be chosen by magic,

as saints and prophets are by gods, as heroes are
by fate, as maidens are by mythic beasts.

But the unicorn did not come to me, and God
did not come to me. In time, love brushed so close

I could smell the beast beyond
the myth of it: lichen and lakebed, salt

and scorch, want that strikes
the back of the throat. Your breath became

a baby's wisps ticking my chin, my nose
unable to resist

falling, again and again, against
her scalp, your chest. The forest

burning closer
like a fuse.

THE CLEARING

My Daughter Talks About the Future

In the big bed where we all sleep,
my daughter asks how she will find her husband,

how her body will tell her when she's in love.
Our ancestors feared futures

that did not come to pass. Though sometimes
what actually happened was worse

than what they feared, in some of those futures
that are already past.

My daughter asks if you always get children
after you get married. *No*, I say, *not always.*

There are so many versions of the future
in movies and on TV. In some of those futures

it is kill or be killed. In some of those futures
I still look like me. This is how I've let my body

soften. My mind. The dusk
is so soft here, this bed,

this child's voice and breath.
I'm half adrift, listening

to my daughter talk about her future
as if tomorrow is a given,

not a gift.

How Babies Are Made

We were walking hard uphill when your aunt said *I guess I'll never get to be a parent,*
and I walked harder, pulled ahead and couldn't see her face when I said she could

always adopt, and then that trailing *if* I have to live with—if the last-
ditch round of chemo didn't kill her, if she survived—and in my periphery,

her hand, snapping the heads off the foxtails. She probably
wanted to break my neck and I don't blame her, and later,

when your father and I were walking up and down
that beach, out of breath with our back and forth—

because I could have gone either way, wasn't
one of those who always knew—she was dead

and we all had to live with that, so
yes, it was out of grief I made you.

CONFESSION: I NEVER WANTED A GARDEN

The women of my family speak flower.
Not bouquet. Not *He loves me! Does he love me?*
Not for decoration or display. They speak flower

as in garden. As in down on their knees, up to their elbows
in dirt, green thumbs calloused and soilsteeped, forearms
torn by thorn. The women of my family speak of flowers

as their wayward children. They say *My,
my, my, I don't know what to do about my Violet.
What am I going to do with my poor Rose?* As in gophers.

As in aphids are devouring her pretty petals. As in sunlight
and rain, toil and prune, and yet sickness, and yet
death. I confess, I love the bulb and bloom

of those names on their tongues—fuchsia, begonia,
gladiola—more than I love the routine of seasons.
I love the weeds as much—mallow, dandelion, clover—

their plain persistence, how lush
a garden greens just before those coddled rows
are overtaken. My grandma was famous for her dahlias

the size of dinner plates. She worked the same patch of dirt
into its feverpitch of flower for over fifty years.
I never wanted a garden, that perennial metaphor

requiring maintenance. I never wanted to stand so still
upon a place that it could mold, like Birkenstocks, to my soles.
So I don't know how I ended up here, saying *my, my,*

mine. My oldest, my baby, my everhungry, swiftgrowing girls.
Maybe it's a language we can't escape if we are lucky
enough to inch closer and closer to old. The terms

change, but there is always the beloved, always our body
between it and the cold. The women of my family ease
arthritic knees onto wooden hassocks, take communion

wafers directly on their tongues. They speak
flower as in oil and smoke to smother the pests,
as in weeds rooted out, relentlessly, ruthlessly.

I don't regret our gardens, only the many wilds
they replace. Whatever we mother, it is tenderly
vicious, this language we speak.

I USED TO DREAM OF FLYING WITH MY EYES

just above the ground, my vision exquisite
with detail. The granules of dirt, the pores

      of stones. To dust off the distance
      of scale is to unearth

an eons old grudge match, territory surrendered
and shaded, inch by inch. The slow entanglement

      of fungi and root. The muffled march of moss.
      I have slept with my cheek against the earth,

my ear crushed between my mind and the soil.
I have listened. I have let the tiny harmless insects

      cover me. I have been afraid and shaken
      webs and wonders from my hair. In dreams

I came so close. Every detail my mind's
invention, but I believed the slow work of me—

      my muscles moving my skull moving my eyes
      my ears my nose and the big greedy skin of me

rolling like a dog in such decadent decay. The ecstasy of looking
through a microscope, without a microscope.

      There are so many worlds to mourn. I haven't
      dreamed of flying for so long. I gaze too hard

at the sky.

Microchimerism: A Proof

If a cloud is an accretion of loosely held molecules,
a person an accretion of loosely held traits.

If rain. If exfoliation, erosion. There are cells
belonging to one who never became, grafted

with the slick of me. And there was a boy who died
just days after our first kiss. What might have been

a blade of shin. A torrential
or unexceptional affair. A vital

organ. I could have held, skin
to skin. Micro: very small in comparison

with others of its kind. Also: too small to be seen
by the unaided eye. The sound *chimera*

evokes a shimmering. Heat rivering
a highway. Film of light on leaves. Fishnet

of webs I have run through. How they cling.
How shining enlarges a thing by blurring

its endings. Imagine the slick of me
as an empty room. If you're not squeamish

about blood, replace *empty* with *haunted* and *room*
with *womb*. Before a house can be sold,

its ghosts must be disclosed.
Because we are willing to believe that walls

can hold. The pillar of cold
in the hallway. The scent of cigarettes.

Of sex. Beware, I mosaic facts to slant
faith into something tangible

that stays. In memory of the dead
boy I kissed once, for only minutes,

I wear the chap of his lips
on my lips. Imagine rain as pollen,

shaken from a lily's elaborate stamen.
If everything it touched stained saffron.

Tell me again how a hurricane ripples
from the single flap

of a morpho butterfly's wings. Sublime,
isn't it, to believe in that, and also that

life exhaled an atmosphere
where it could breathe? Life meaning virus,

but also me. See this bruise fading
on my thigh? I can't recall the corner

I collided with, but must have left some skin
cells there. How long do cells live,

if they are never born? Why not forever.
Why not everywhere.

Transfusion

My daughter's blood thins as it weaves
through her spleen, so we enter the land of illness,
settle in like tourists in a warplagued nation,
sure the bombs will fall, but not on us.

My daughter is ten months old
so I have to nurse her
to keep her still while they insert
the IV. So she screams and sucks,

sucks and screams, learning sustenance
is this, but also this. My daughter's wrist
is splinted, bandaged, so she cannot unbind
herself from this reverse bleeding. So

her body accepts the needle, the thread
of blood that stitches her to wellness. So this
blood will propel her through health's wilds
until it too is burnt away. So oxygen

circulates with the clattering carts, the weak
coffee, the hanging bladders of sugar and saline.
So we wait behind the plastic curtain, watch
cuffs and big and little soles brisk past

as if everyone but us is cut off
at the shins. So we listen to the whimpers
of children we can't see, soft hushes
of their hidden parents. But I do see them

when I take my turn to pace the length
of our ward. Some are like my daughter,
dual citizens of sickness and health.
Others are here for chemo, health a land of gold-

paved roads they've only heard of, never known.
So I want to describe these children, their clear-
cut foreheads, their eyes like oilskinned lakes
only God could have set ablaze. So I'm tempted

to say angelic, otherworldly. So I learn how far
I am from compassion. From inhabiting
another's life. So my daughter takes
the blood of another and grows bright

with it. She glistens a health that nearly sickens
in this place where others take and take into
their bodies whatever they are told and still
they pale and pale unto translucence. So

some of these children will die
taking the cancer with them. Still,
we get hungry, and the cafeteria is a copy
of a café, the sandwich a kind of food

we might enjoy in different light. So night
and these halls fill like boulevards
in liberated cities, where even the shellshocked
come out to stroll in evening. So the glass doors

part. So we leave, burn a little upon reentry
into this blessed dusk. The sidewalk
sparked with mica, pines pixelated
with wind, glittering

impossibly. So it's still possible
to feel the day rising up from the asphalt,
a heat our legs swing through as if through
a field. It's still possible to fall into our car

as if across the back of an old mare
who knows the way home. Or better yet,
to a new place where we can pitch a life
beneath some abandoned plot of sky, overgrown

with stars, where we can believe luck really is
common and tarnished as a penny. So we pocket it
unashamed, knowing it can buy us nothing
but the moment of its gleam.

Time Capsule: The Poem

I want the poem to hold everything the way my body holds
the whole and holy of me. The way the body holds both

bile duct and silver snaps of synapse. The way the brain holds both
reptile and godglow, both fight or flight and dreams

of flying.
I want the poem to hold the way my mind holds

my hand on the wheel and the war
on the radio and the distance

between bombs and borders. Bodies
and ash. I want this poem to hold the dead.

Both mine and ours. And the future
that is tomorrow and the tomorrow

we won't live to see. I want this poem to hold the way one moment holds
both the beloved and the trees outside as they ring

a new year, in which another language disappears. Rain on a roof
or something softer. The way all hard things soften in death into what

surrounds them. The way our bodies soften
into each other.

The way love holds both time and no other clock
but the *soft soft soft* of rain.

The way the clock chimes now
and now holds both here, a body burning with desire, and there,

a forest on fire. And above us, all the stars.

And within us all, the stars. I want this poem to hold space
and to hold a space

for you to fill

after it fails.

Time Capsule: The Fossil Record

Twilight. A river rock, smooth in my palm. A river

canyoning a meadow with the consistency

of its leaving. Some fossil sea always beneath.

Science has yet to raise the dead.

Still, I flesh each bone, as if I remember.

It has been years since my bare feet blued

in that current of snowmelt, since the rock

I pocketed lost its shine, became mine.

It has been eons since I touched

the one I stood there with. There is so much

to miss. Stone in my hand, river in my mind.

Sometimes, in the shallows of sleep,

my whole skin senses a warm, familiar sea.

A sense that something far too large to love

me holds me anyway. A different way to spar

with gravity. Each metatarsal holds

the glacial cold, my mind the cloud

of minnows shattered by my footsteps.

Stone in my hand, river

through my fingers.

Caesura

I remember hearing about them, the babies   my grandma never had,
and though I'd never held such a seed   in my body, I felt the want
of them. Five children with ghostspaces   between. She believed
unbaptized souls went to Limbo,   which to me meant low,
so I saw them spread like mica   in the soil beneath her roses,
and in the gauze of grasshoppers   that rose with every step
through summer grass.   On my grandma's ranch, I watched
a barn cat lick her living kittens   clean, leaving some still
sacked. Little grapes, their mother's   warmth unreplaced by their own.
When I bled, I locked the bathroom door.   Later, I pressed a still-
frame of my only ultrasound inside   my grandma's copy
of *The Secret Garden*. Little unblossom,   little mausoleum.
I'm not religious anymore, but I grew up   with God,
the grandfatherly one who knew I was bad   sometimes,
but loved me anyway, and I could always talk to.   It's a hard habit
to break in the cathedral of my sleeping daughters,   that consecrated dark
gauzed in white noise, a halo of nightlight.   My prayers are always
some variation of *Don't you dare*, and *Please*.   Somehow, I know he was a boy.
The middle brother. So little now,   so nothing. My daughters don't know
the word *God*. They know earth and death   and rain. They've watched
that silent sleight of hand replace   a caterpillar with an iridescent bud
of wings. They've seen me clutch   a spider between paper and a plastic cup,
only to crush a mosquito against   their bedroom wall, its body smeared
with our family's mingled blood.   They are learning to be merciful
doesn't mean to be good, only powerful   enough to choose.
After our cat died my oldest kept asking   *Where is she? I know she's dead*
but where is she? First, I spun a heavenplace,   then I changed my mind,
stood her barefoot in the garden and said   *Here, look down.*
The dirt is full of root and bone.   Oh, my darlings, we are so small.
Lie down, back to summer grass. Feel   how we are always falling
into that starspread black expanse.   And feel too
the way the earth holds us,   and we are held.

WHILE HUNTING MUMMIES AT THE MUSEUM

my daughter asks *When someone dies*
will you help me make an altar? and I wonder
if she's made some kind of peace
with the vast incomprehensible

that laps our lives. Between her question
and my *Sure* there is a long shushsigh.
Some call this the word, others the lie.
I call it the reason love is laced always

with a stunning sadness. This mummy,
so unlike the cartoon version she expected,
no bandages trailing, only flesh
so long dead it's shrinkwrapped

unrecognizable, to pelvis, to skull.
When she is older, I will make her promise
to bury me naked, unbound. I want to vanish
quick. But right now, she wants to understand

a thing by repetition, even the dead.
She demands another and another
until there are no bodies left.
I imagine dirt dissolving

this body that birthed her. Her hand,
still so small in mine, as we try not to lose
each other in the crowd gathered
around the childsized mummy.

And because I might be vague
about the Tooth Fairy
and Santa, but swore I'd never lie
I have to say *Yes*

when she wonders, inevitably,
if she too will die. The next
sarcophagus is empty, so I myth
it with a mummy, bandage-

wrapped and risen, then make
the promise, that is, at best,
only half mine to keep:
But baby, not for a long, long time.

Acknowledgments

Thanks to the editors of the publications where the following poems first appeared, sometimes in earlier versions:

The Adroit Journal – "Time Capsule: The Uneven Field" and "I was the girl who jumped first"

Blackbird – "Maybe It Was Summer" and "While hunting mummies at the museum"

Bracken – "The poem begins with us surviving"

Cider Press Review – "Huntress"

Connotation Press – "Transfusion"

EcoTheo Review – "The Last Mother" and "Eve, Alone"

Fairy Tale Review – "Oh Artemis,"

FERAL: A Journal of Poetry and Art – "Time Capsule: The Poem"

Montreal International Poetry Prize Global Anthology 2017 – "Caesura" (winning poem)

Muzzle Magazine – "Time Capsule: The Fallow Deer"

Ninth Letter – "Lullaby with Fireflies and Rising Seas" (winner of the 2017 Literary Award)

Pinwheel – "Immolation Lessons"

Poetry Northwest – "Growing Up Wild," "Test," and "Microchimerism: A Proof"

Rise Up Review – "My Daughter Talks About the Future"

The Rumpus – "Preservation Lessons"

The Shore – "Time Capsule: Days of Ash from Elsewhere"

The West Review – "On Being Out of the Woods" and "Forgive me, I've forgotten"

This book would not exist without so many different kinds of support I've received from so many generous people.

I want to begin by thanking Michael Waters for believing in this book, and Ron Mitchell for refining and shaping it into the best possible version of itself. Thank you to everyone at SIR Press, I can't imagine a more perfect home for this collection.

Thank you to Marilyn Chin, Vandana Khanna, Dean Rader, and Michael Waters for blessing this book with your words.

Thank you to Chie Yoshii for allowing her stunning painting to grace my cover, and to Suz Lipman for making my author photo shoot among the redwoods so easy and fun.

Thank you to Lynne Knight for being the first reader of the manuscript that became this book. You gave me the encouragement I needed to start the daunting process of submitting it.

Thank you to Carly Joy Miller, my poet sister, for being the first reader of so many of these poems. You always show me the possibilities in language, where it all begins.

Thank you to my brilliant mentor, Thomas Centolella, and the Mill Valley writing group: Ella Eytan, Suzanne Himmelwright, Leta Bushyhead, Jennifer Nichols, Suz Lipman, Angelika Quirk, and Edward Marson. You all keep my poems honest.

Thank you to all the teachers and mentors who have given me the gift of their wisdom and guidance over the years: Sandra Alcosser, Ilya Kaminsky, Marilyn Chin, Shadab Zeest Hashmi, Gabrielle Calvocoressi, Kate Gale, Piotr Florczyk, Jenny Minniti-Shippey, Meagan Marshall, Julie Bruck, Matthew Lippman, and Steve Kowit.

Thank you to the members of Sixteen Rivers Press, the board of the Marin Poetry Center, and the teachers and students at the Writing Salon for being my Bay Area poetry community.

Thank you to the friends and colleagues who have promoted my work, invited me into opportunities, cheered me on, and inspired me in countless ways: Daniela Sow, Kevin Dublin, Francine Rockey, Tara Stillions Whitehead, Carrie Moniz, Rachel Gellman-Martin, Erica Curtis, Danielle Hunt, Jenna D'Anna, Susan Hogan, Kaitlin Dyer, Scott Stewart, Nicole Bartolini, Helen Lee, Serreta Martin, Lisa Grove, Jen Lagendrost Cavender, Georgina Marie, Annette Robichaud, Laura Praytor, Pawel Samolewicz, Lee Rankin, the Slades, and so many others in other countries and other lives. If I ever loved you, even if we don't really know each other anymore, I still love you.

To Yatindra, this book would never have been written without the hikes, beach days, and bike rides you took the kids on. I know how very blessed we are to have found and kept each other. To my daughters, Kavya and Leela, you keep me open to the world of magic and imagination, you are my greatest inspiration.

Thank you to my parents for always being there for me in too many ways to list, and for teaching me to value wilderness and wild creatures. And to my brother for exploring the woods and meadows of childhood with me, thank you for your lifelong friendship. Thank you to my whole extended family for the backyard feasts, games, and laughter as the fog rolled in.

Thank you to those I've lost who haunt and light these pages.

And lastly, thank you to my tree and all the others for holding all our breaths.

The Michael Waters Poetry Prize was established in 2013 to honor Michael's contributions to *Southern Indiana Review* and American arts and letters.

MWPP Winners

2020 — Erin Rodoni

2019 — Julia Koets

2018 — Chelsea Wagenaar

2017 — Marty McConnell

2016 — Ruth Awad

2015 — Annie Kim

2014 — Dennis Hinrichsen & Hannah Faith Notess

2013 — Doug Ramspeck

Southern Indiana Review Press